The Old House

Ron Holt

1 A house in the country

Adam Green is eight. He has a sister, Lisa. She's older. She's eleven. Adam and Lisa have a parrot. His name is Joe. He's on his perch.

Adam and Lisa live in a small flat in the town. Their mother is in the kitchen. She's talking to her husband.

'I don't like this flat,' says Mrs Green. 'It's too small. Look at this kitchen. It's very small. I'd like a bigger one.'

'You're right,' says Mr Green. 'This flat is too small. I'm going to look for a bigger one.'

He stands up and knocks Joe the parrot off his perch.

'Eeerk!' says Joe. 'Too small! Too small!'

The Green family are looking in an estate agent's window. An estate agent sells houses and flats.

'Look at that house,' says Mr Green.

'Which one?' asks Mrs Green.

'The one on the hill,' says Mr Green.

'It's very old,' says Mrs Green.

'I can fix it up,' says Mr Green. 'It has a big living room, a very big kitchen and three bedrooms. What do you think, kids?'

'I like it,' says Lisa. 'It's in the country. I don't like the city. The air is too dirty.'

'It's great,' says Adam. 'Look, there's a pond at the bottom of the hill. I can go fishing.'

'Let's go and see it,' says Mr Green.

The Green family are in their car. They're going to look at the house.

'Look at the streets,' says Lisa. 'There's litter everywhere. Why do people drop litter? Why don't they put it in the litter bins?'

'There isn't any litter in the country,' says Adam. 'And the air is cleaner.'

'The air isn't clean here,' says Lisa. 'Look at the smoke coming from that lorry. Where's Joe? I can't see him because of the smoke.'

The car leaves the city.

'That's better,' says Mr Green. 'There's less traffic now.'

'I like the country,' says Mrs Green.

'Eeerk!' says Joe. 'I like it! I like it!'

'Where's the house?' asks Lisa.

'We turn left,' says Mr Green. 'The house is on the right. It's on a hill.'

'There's the hill!' says Lisa.

'There's the pond,' says Adam.

'And there's the house,' says Mr Green.

'Oh,' says Mrs Green. 'It's very old.'

The car stops in front of the house and the children jump out. Adam runs down to the pond and Joe flies after him.

'The pond's full of rubbish,' shouts Adam.

'Rubbish! Rubbish!' says Joe.

'Never mind,' says Mr Green. 'We can clean it out. Let's look at the house.'

They go into the kitchen.

'It's big,' says Mr Green.

'Oh!' says Mrs Green. 'There isn't any water. The sink doesn't have any taps!'

'The house has electricity,' says Mr Green. 'There should be water.'

Mr Green goes into the yard.

'Here's the water,' shouts Mr Green. 'We can get water from this well.'

'There isn't a bathroom,' says Mrs Green.

'I can build one,' answers Mr Green. 'I can put water in the house. Don't worry. I can do it.'

'Are we going to buy the house?' asks Adam.

'I don't know,' says Mr Green. 'Your mother doesn't like it.'

'I do like it,' says Mrs Green. 'It only needs a new bathroom.'

'OK,' says Mr Green. 'Let's buy the old house.'

The family are working on the old house. Mr Green is building a bathroom. There's a new water tank on the roof. There are taps in the kitchen sink. Mrs Green is painting the kitchen and Lisa is helping her.

Adam is cleaning out the pond. There is a lot of rubbish in it. Adam is pulling an old bike from the water. Joe stands on it. Lisa comes to the pond.

'Can I help you, Adam?' she asks. 'I don't like painting.'

'OK,' replies Adam. 'Can you see that pile of rubbish near the house? Put this old bike on it. Joe! Move!'

Adam pulls an old bed from the pond.

'Why do people throw rubbish into ponds?' he complains.

2 The farmer

'Well,' says Adam, 'it's clean now.'

'And we have a big pile of rubbish,' says Lisa. 'Are there any fish in the pond?'

'No, there aren't,' answers Adam. 'I wonder why.'

'Look!' says Lisa. 'A stream runs into the pond. Perhaps the stream is dirty.'

'Let's find out,' says Adam.

Adam and Lisa walk along the stream. They come to a farm where there are some ducks, hens and cows. The farmer is washing out the cowshed.

'Where does the dirty water go?' asks Adam.

'It goes into the stream,' says Lisa.

'Then it goes into our pond,' says Adam. 'That's why the pond is dirty.'

Adam and Lisa walk to the cowshed.

'Hello,' says the farmer. 'Who are you?'

'Hello. I'm Adam Green,' replies Adam, 'and this is my sister, Lisa.'

'Where do you live?' asks the farmer.

'We live in the old house,' Lisa replies.

'Is that the old house near the pond?' asks the farmer.

'That's right,' says Adam.

'There aren't any fish in the pond,' says Lisa. 'The water is too dirty.'

'Eeerk!' says Joe. 'Too dirty! Too dirty!'

'And why is that?' asks the farmer.

'The dirty water from your cowshed runs into the stream. The stream runs into the pond,' says Adam.

'I'm sorry,' says the farmer. 'That's why there aren't any fish in your pond. I must do something about it.'

The next day a big digger comes to the farm. Lisa and Adam are watching it.

'What is it doing?' asks Lisa.

'It's digging a big hole,' says Adam.

'Hello,' says the farmer. 'Can you see what I'm doing?'

'Yes,' replies Adam. 'It's for the dirty water.'

'That's right,' says the farmer. 'We mustn't spoil our streams and rivers. Your pond is going to be all right now.'

Adam and Lisa walk back along the stream. The water is clean now. They come to the pond.

'Are there any fish?' asks Lisa.

'Not yet,' replies Adam. 'We must be patient.'

'Be patient! Be patient!' says Joe.

Adam and Lisa aren't patient. They look at the pond every day.

'Can you see any fish?' asks Lisa.

'No, I can't,' says Adam. 'The water is clean now but there aren't any fish.'

Mr Green calls to the children.

'Come and help us,' he says. 'Peter is here with his lorry.'

Peter is Mr Green's friend. His lorry is near the big pile of rubbish.

'Where's all this rubbish from?' asks Peter.

'It's from the house and the pond,' replies Mr Green. 'Now kids, put the rubbish in three piles. Put the old bike and the metal things here. Put the bottles there. Leave the rest here.'

The children sort out the rubbish; their father and Peter put it on the lorry. They drive to a big yard. There are some big rubbish skips in the yard.

'Put the old bike and the metal things in that skip,' says Mr Green. He points to the skip marked 'metal'. Then they throw the bottles in the second skip. 'Throw the rest in here,' says Mr Green.

'What will happen to all this rubbish?' asks Adam.

'They're going to recycle it,' says Peter.

'What does that mean?' asks Lisa.

'It means they'll make new bottles and new metal things,' says Mr Green.

'Eeerk!' says Joe. 'Recycle! Recycle!'

3 A box in the cellar

Mrs Green is very happy. She is in her new kitchen. She has a new bathroom and there's plenty of water.

'How do you like the old house now?' asks Mr Green.

'I love it,' says Mrs Green. 'It's bigger than our old flat. The air is cleaner and the children are happier. I'm happier too.'

'I'm going to do the cellar,' says Mr Green. The cellar is the room under the house.

'What's in the cellar?' asks Mrs Green.

'Nothing now,' answers Mr Green. 'There is no floor. I'm going to put a new floor in it. Then I'm going to paint it.'

Adam and Lisa go down into the cellar with their father. He switches on the light. The cellar is very big.

'It's bigger than the living room,' says Adam. 'We can play in here.'

'I'm going to buy a ping pong table,' says Mr Green. 'We can put it in here. But we must have a new floor first.'

'What can we do?' asks Adam.

'The floor must be flat,' says Mr Green. 'Then I'm going to put tiles on it. You can put that rubbish in the bucket. Here's the spade.'

'Eeerk!' says Joe. 'Rubbish! Rubbish!'

Mr Green starts to put tiles on the floor. Lisa sweeps the floor. Adam puts the rubbish in the bucket.

'Where do I put this rubbish?' he asks.

'Take it outside,' answers his father.

Adam takes the bucket of rubbish outside and comes back into the cellar.

'I'm tired,' he says.

Lisa picks up the spade and puts the rest of the rubbish in the bucket.

'Now you can sweep the floor, Adam,' she says.

Adam picks up the brush and sweeps the floor.

'What's Joe doing?' asks Lisa, pointing to the parrot.

'I don't know,' says Adam. 'He's scratching something. Give me the spade.' Adam scrapes the floor.

'It's a box,' says Adam. 'Dad! Come here.'

Mr Green is putting tiles on the floor.

'What is it?' he asks.

'It's a metal box,' says Adam. 'It's in the ground.'

Mr Green takes the spade and digs the box out of the ground. He tries to open it.

'I can't open it,' he says. 'Let's take it upstairs.'

Adam and Lisa carry the box upstairs.

'It's heavy,' says Lisa. 'I wonder what's in it.'

They take the box into the kitchen and put it on the table.

'The box is very old,' says Mr Green. He picks up a screwdriver and opens it.

'What's in it?' asks Adam impatiently.

'Money,' says Mr Green. 'Some old coins.'

'Eeerk!' says Joe. 'Money! Money!'

'Can I buy a bike?' says Adam.

'No,' says Mr Green. 'We can't spend these coins. They're very old.'

'What are we going to do with them?' says Lisa.

'We're going to take them to the museum,' says her father. 'I'll phone the museum.'

Mr Green and the children are in the car. They're driving to the museum. They pass factories and shops. There's a lot of traffic on the road. Mr Green parks his car near the museum.

Adam and Lisa carry the box into the museum. A man is sitting behind a desk near the door.

'Mr Brass, please,' says Mr Green.

'Second door on the right,' answers the man. 'Mr Brass is in his room.'

Adam and Lisa carry the box to Mr Brass's room. Mr Green knocks on the door. Mr Brass opens it.

'Come in, Mr Green,' he says.

Mr Brass puts the coins carefully on his desk.

'How many are there?' he asks.

'Two hundred and thirty-three,' says Adam.

Mr Brass looks at the coins. 'Mmmm . . .,' he says. 'Excellent. Mmmm . . . Very good. Mmm . . .'

'Well,' says Mr Green. 'Are they real? Are they old?'

'Be patient,' says Mr Brass.

Mr Brass takes a thick book from his bookcase. He turns the pages of the book.

'Mmmm . . .,' he says. 'I can answer your questions now, Mr Green. The coins are real. They are old. They are two hundred years old.'

'And the metal?' says Mr Green. 'What are they made of?'

'Some are silver,' says Mr Brass. 'Some are gold.'

'Eeerk!' says Joe. 'Gold! Gold!'

The next day, Mr Green opens his newspaper.

Children find coins in old house

'It's in the paper,' he shouts.

'What's in the paper?' says Lisa.

'Listen!' says Mr Green, reading the paper. 'Children find coins in old house.'

There is a knock at the door.

'Answer the door, Adam,' says Mr Green.

Adam goes to the door and opens it. He comes back with a man.

'I'm Sam Spice,' says the man. 'I'm a reporter on the *Oldtown News*. Can you answer some questions for me, please?'

'OK,' says Mr Green. 'What do you want to know?'

'Tell me about the coins,' says Sam.

'Sit down,' says Mrs Green. 'Would you like some coffee?'

'Please,' says Sam.

Sam Spice drinks his coffee.

'Very nice,' he says. 'Now, Mr Green, tell me about the coins.'

'Well,' says Mr Green. 'They're gold and silver coins.'

'How much are they worth?' asks Sam.

'I don't know,' says Mr Green. 'The museum is going to keep them. They're going to pay us one thousand pounds.'

'Very good,' says Sam. 'And what are you going to do with the money?'

'We're going to buy some things for the house,' says Mr Green.

'What do you say, kids?' says Sam.

'Fantastic!' say Adam and Lisa.

'Eeerk!' says Joe. 'Fantastic!'

The old house looks beautiful. The windows and doors have new paint. They are green and white. The garden has beautiful flowers and vegetables, and some apple trees. Lisa and Mrs Green are picking flowers. Mr Green is picking strawberries. He puts them in a basket and gives them to Lisa. Mrs Green and Lisa go into the kitchen.

'What are we going to have for supper?' asks Lisa.

'Salad sandwiches and cake,' says Mrs Green.

'And strawberries and cream,' says Lisa.

'Of course,' says her mother.

'Of course,' says Joe.

Adam is fishing in the pond. It's very clean now. There are some trees round it and two ducks are swimming on it. Adam has a new fishing rod. He puts a worm on his hook.

'Shoo!' he shouts to the ducks and they fly away.

Adam's father comes to the pond.

'Are there any fish in it yet?' he asks.

'I don't know,' says Adam.

Suddenly Adam's fishing rod bends and Joe flies into the air. 'Eeerk!' he cries.

'It's a fish!' Adam shouts.

'Nice one!' says his father. 'Are you going to eat it?'

Adam doesn't answer. He takes the fish off the hook and puts it back in the pond.

Questions

Chapter 1
1 How old is Adam?
2 Who is Lisa?
3 What would Mrs Green like?
4 Where are the Greens?
5 Why doesn't Lisa like the city?
6 Where is the air clean?
7 Does Mrs Green like the house?
8 Why do you think people throw rubbish into ponds?
9 Punctuate this sentence:
well says adam its clean now

Chapter 2
1 Why aren't there any fish in the pond?
2 What is the farmer doing?
3 Why is the stream dirty?
4 Where is the rubbish from?
5 How many skips are there?
6 What are they going to do with the rubbish?
7 What do you do with your rubbish?

8 Punctuate this sentence:
are there any fish in the pond

Chapter 3
1 Why is Mrs Green happy?
2 What is a cellar?
3 What is Mr Green going to do?
4 What is Mr Green going to buy?
5 What does Adam put in the bucket?
6 Why is Adam tired?
7 What does Lisa see?
8 What is in the box?
9 Where do the Greens go?
10 How old are the coins?
11 Who comes to the house?
12 Who is going to have the coins?
13 What are the Greens going to do with the money?
14 What would you do with the money?
15 What is Adam doing?
16 Why does Adam put the fish back in the pond?
17 Would you put the fish back in the pond? Why?

The Town Child

I live in the town
In a street;
It is crowded with traffic
And feet;
There are buses and motors[1]
And trams;
I wish there were meadows
And lambs.

The houses all wait
In a row.
There is smoke everywhere
That I go.
I don't hear the noises
I hear —
I wish there were woods
Very near.

There is only one thing
That I love,
And that is the sky
Far above.
There is plenty of room
In the blue
For castles of clouds
And me, too!

Irene Thompson

1 *motors* cars

The Country Child

My home is a house
    Near a wood
(I'd live in a street
    If I could!)
The lanes are so quiet,
    Oh, dear!
I do wish that someone
    Lived near.

There is no one to play with
    At all.
The trees are so high
    And so tall:
And I should be lonely
    For hours,
Were it not for the birds
    And the flowers.

I wish that I lived
    In a town —
To see all the trams
    Going down
A twinkling street
    That is bright
With wonderful colours
    At night.

Irene Thompson

Find the words

There are 21 words from the story in the box below. Can you find them? They are down and across. Use all the letters. Use some letters twice.

p	a	r	r	o	t	h	i	l	l
m	s	i	l	v	e	r		i	
u	g		b	u	c	k	e	t	
s	o		l	c		c	i	t	y
e	l	r	o	o	f	e	p	e	c
u	d	f	r	w	a	l	o	r	o
m	d	l	r	s	r	l	n	f	i
b	u	o	y		m	a	d	i	n
o	c	o	u	n	t	r	y	s	s
x	k	r	u	b	b	i	s	h	

Write the words here:

_____   _____   _____

_____   _____   _____

_____   _____   _____

_____   _____   _____

_____   _____   _____

_____   _____   _____

_____   _____   _____

Rubbish is useful

Every day we throw away many kilos of rubbish. But did you know that a lot of this rubbish is still useful?

Recycling

Metal, glass, paper and even plastic can be used again. They can be 'recycled'.

In many countries, rubbish has been recycled for a long time. The 'zabbaleen' in Egypt are very good at recycling most of the rubbish which they collect. They sort out the rubbish into piles of plastic, tin, glass, cardboard, paper, bottle tops and so on. They find a use for most of these. Sometimes they turn them into other useful things.

In Europe, less rubbish is used again because recycling is expensive. But it is becoming easier and cheaper. People are now collecting things to be recycled. For example, many people do not throw away empty bottles. They take them to 'bottle banks'. The broken bottles are collected. They are then used to make new bottles.

Paper is also used again. It is used to make 'recycled paper'. This is very important.

When we use recycled paper, we help to save trees. In one year a family throws away about 50 kilos of paper. It takes about six trees to make 50 kilos of paper.

Trees are important to our planet. We use too much paper and we throw away too much paper. Every day, many trees are cut down. The areas are left bare. They are no good for farming. Soon there will not be enough good land for people to live on.

Using rubbish for energy

If rubbish cannot be recycled, it can be used to make energy. Burning rubbish makes energy. It is cheaper and cleaner than burning oil. But only a small amount of rubbish is used to make energy. Most rubbish is still thrown away or buried underground.

Recycling rubbish is better than throwing it away. Why?
Because:
- it saves money,
- it saves energy,
- it makes more energy,
- it saves trees,
- it makes less pollution.

Art and Science

Christine Fleming

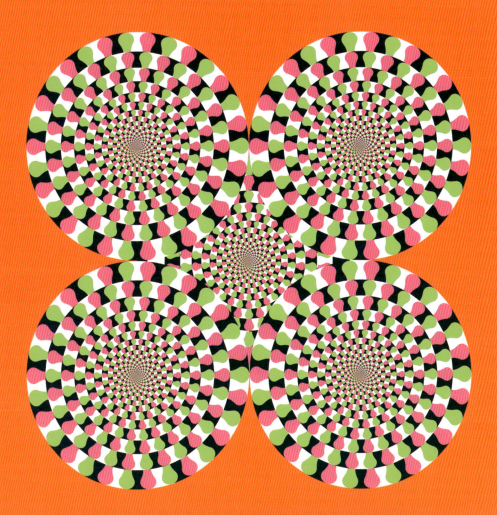

SCHOLASTIC

This 2010 British adaptation published by
Scholastic Ltd
Villiers House
Clarendon Avenue
Leamington Spa
Warwickshire CV32 5PR

British Library Cataloguing-in-Publication Data.
A catalogue record for this book is available from the British Library.
ISBN 978-1407-11339-5

© 2009 Weldon Owen Pty Ltd. All rights reserved.

Author: Christine Fleming
Educational Consultants: Ian Morrison and Nikki Gamble
Editors: Mary Atkinson, Marion Archer and Simret Brar
Designer: Carol Hsu
Photo Researchers: Jamshed Mistry and Sarah Matthewson

Photographs by: AGE, W.Bibikow/www.stockcentral.co.nz (pp. 6–7); **Anne Luo** (p. 1; p. 5; fractal, pp. 22–23; op-art circles, p. 25); **Jennifer and Brian Lupton** (p. 30; girl pointing, p. 31); **Getty Images** (dancers, sculptor, p. 9; weaver, p. 13; cave art, pp. 14–15; Egyptian stone cat, p. 20; Han van Meegeren trial, p. 21; science photographer, p. 29); **© 2007 The M. C. Escher Company-Holland. All rights reserved. www.mcescher.com** (M. C. Escher's *Convex and Concave*, 1955 Lithograph, cover; M. C. Escher's symmetry drawing E103, pp. 22–23; M. C. Escher's *Waterfall*, 1961, pp. 24–25); **National Geographic Image Collection** (skull holograms, p. 27); **Photolibrary** (Leon Battista Alberti, p. 8; Sphinx, p. 14; X-ray of Titian painting, p. 18; infrared scanner, p. 19; forgery, p. 21; music score, p. 28); **Stock.Xchng** (clogs, p. 13; pyramid, pp. 10–11); **Tranz/Corbis** (church, p. 8; columns, p. 10; Rupmati Pavilion, Hypobank, p. 11; p. 12; Sistine Chapel restoration, p. 15; *Bacchus and Ariadne*, pigment pot, p. 17; conservator at work, pp. 18–19; mandala, p. 23; *Vega-Nor*, p. 24; still from *Final Fantasy*, pp. 26–27; Jacqueline Kennedy Onassis, p. 27; making digital music, pp. 28–29; photographer, p. 29; girl with microscope, pp. 30–31) **© RayPics / Alamy** (Fractal, cover)

Every effort has been made to trace copyright holders for the works reproduced in this book, and the publishers apologise for any inadvertent omissions.

All other illustrations and photographs © Weldon Owen Pty Ltd.

All rights reserved. This book is sold subject to the condition that it shall not, by way of trade or otherwise, be lent, hired out or otherwise circulated without the publisher's prior consent in any form of binding or cover other than that in which it is published and without a similar condition, including this condition, being imposed upon the subsequent purchaser. No part of this publication may be produced, stored in a retrieval system, or transmitted, in any form or by any means, electronic, mechanical, photocopying, recording or otherwise, other than for the purposes described in the lessons in this book, without the prior permission of the publisher. This book remains in copyright, although permission is granted to copy pages where indicated for classroom distribution and use only in the school which has purchased the book, or by the teacher who has purchased the book, and in accordance with the CLA licensing agreement. Photocopying permission is given only for purchasers and not borrowers of books from any lending service.

Due to the nature of the web, we cannot guarantee the content or links of any site mentioned. We strongly recommend that teachers check websites before using them in the classroom.

Teachers' notes contain extracts from Primary National Strategy's Primary Framework for Literacy (2006) www.standards.dfes.gov.uk/primaryframework © Crown copyright. Reproduced under the terms of the Click Use Licence.

1 2 3 4 5 6 7 8 9   0 1 2 3 4 5 6 7 8 9

Printed in China through Colorcraft Ltd., Hong Kong

CONTENTS

HIGH-POWERED WORDS	4
GET ON THE WAVELENGTH	6
Master the Art	8
Shaping Up	10
Everyday Art	12
Ancient Art, Modern Science	14
Pigment and Paint	16
The Tools of the Trade	18
Fake!	20
Art and Maths	22
The Art of Illusion	24
Technology and Art	26
Music and Much More	28
AFTERSHOCKS	30
GLOSSARY	32
INDEX	32

Samoan pattern on bark cloth

HIGH-POWERED WORDS

architect a person who designs buildings

canvas a piece of fabric on which an artist paints

commission to hire someone to do a particular piece of work

fractal an image created using a maths formula. A fractal consists of a pattern that repeats itself on smaller and smaller scales.

perspective the art of drawing or painting a scene so that forms and objects appear to have the same shapes and relative sizes as they do in real life. For example, distant objects are smaller than nearer ones.

pigment a richly coloured substance that is used to impart colour to other materials

sculpture a piece of art carved or shaped out of a material such as stone, wood, clay or metal

tessellation a pattern created out of geometric shapes that fit together without any gaps

....

For easy reference, see Wordmark on back flap.
For additional vocabulary, see Glossary on page 32.

> The word *tessellation* comes from *tessera*, the Greek root for *four*. A tessera is a small, often square, tile used in a mosaic. When many tesserae are put together, they become a tessellation.

GET ON THE WAVELENGTH

Today, most people think of art and science as separate subjects, but they are related. Some of the greatest minds have combined creative and scientific ideas. In the 1400s, Leonardo da Vinci studied the human body to make his paintings more realistic. He went on to produce outstanding artworks. He also made some important scientific discoveries.

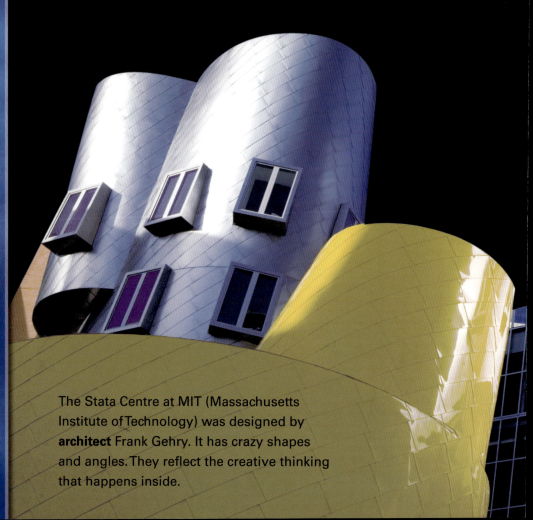

The Stata Centre at MIT (Massachusetts Institute of Technology) was designed by **architect** Frank Gehry. It has crazy shapes and angles. They reflect the creative thinking that happens inside.

Thinking to do with science and maths takes place mainly in our brain's left side. Thinking to do with art and other creative subjects takes place mainly in our brain's right side. There are many ways that we can use both halves of our brains to produce exciting results. Many creative people, such as architects, have jobs with science or maths content. Some people, such as art **restorers**, use science to save works of art.

Master the Art

When we talk about the arts, we usually mean such things as painting, **sculpture** and music. However, this was not always the case. In the past, the arts included any skill that someone had mastered. People who studied art in **Renaissance** times learned languages, maths and music. They also learned science, painting, sculpture and architecture.

Leon Battista Alberti lived in Renaissance Italy. He excelled in maths, architecture, painting, poetry and sports. He was what we now call a Renaissance m...

This church in Italy was designed by Alberti in 1470.

Santa Ma... Novella, Florence, Italy

We need special talent to do well in some arts. We call these the fine arts. Painting, drama and literature are fine arts. The purpose of a fine art is mainly to give pleasure. It is also to pass on ideas. Other arts are called useful arts. These include cooking and weaving. They have an everyday purpose. However, they also allow people to express their creativity.

Some artists earn their living from their work. For many others, art is a hobby. They enjoy being creative. However, they may not wish to make art their profession.

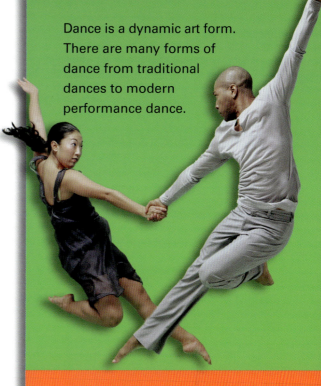

Dance is a dynamic art form. There are many forms of dance from traditional dances to modern performance dance.

We use the term *master the art* for just about any skill. We say, "She has mastered the art of playing the guitar." Here we are using the word *art* to mean a highly developed skill.

Sculpture is a fine art. It allows artists to express their **traditions** and their own ideas.

Shaping Up

Throughout history, powerful rulers have hired talented architects. The architects have designed palaces, tombs and public buildings. They have used science and maths to ensure their buildings are strong and practical. They have used their artistic skills to design enduring **masterpieces**.

Many of the shapes chosen by architects have a practical purpose. Rows of columns allow walls to be lightweight. Curved arches can support greater weights than straight beams. Domed roofs are stronger than flat roofs.

This Mayan pyramid was built around AD1200. It has 365 steps.

Pyramid of Kukulkan, Mexico

In 1988, a glass pyramid was built in the courtyard of the French art gallery, The Louvre. Use the internet to find images and information about this impressive building, which combines science and art in its construction.

Pyramids are strong, stable structures. In ancient times, architects chose pyramids as tombs for their greatest rulers. They knew that a huge stone pyramid would last thousands of years.

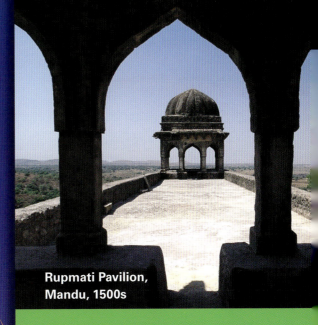

Rupmati Pavilion, Mandu, 1500s

Many Indian palaces have arches, domes and columns.

SHOCKER

In the 1200s, architects in Europe competed to build the highest **cathedral**. The contest ended in 1284. That was when Beauvais Cathedral in France collapsed. It had been about 53 metres high.

Hypobank building, Munich, Germany

This building has distinctive columns. They look as if they are held onto the building with giant clamps.

11

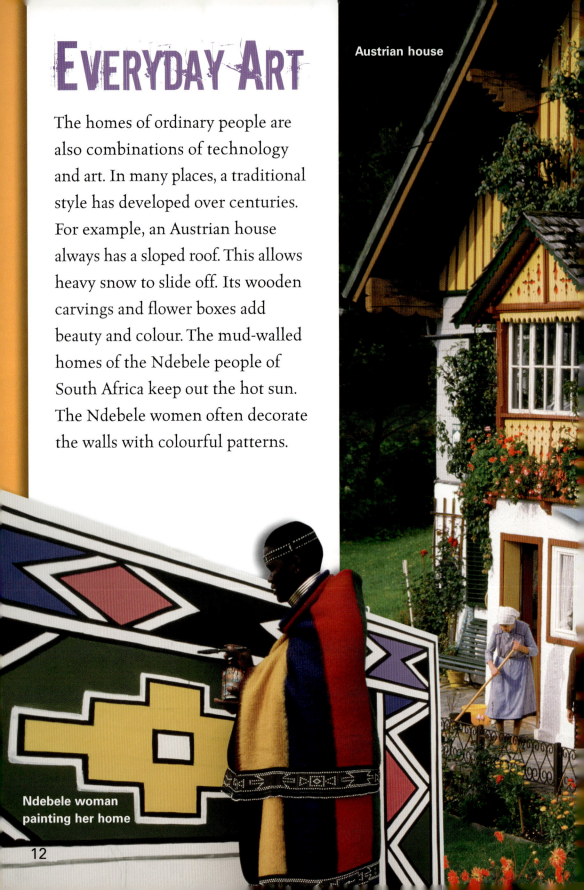

EVERYDAY ART

Austrian house

The homes of ordinary people are also combinations of technology and art. In many places, a traditional style has developed over centuries. For example, an Austrian house always has a sloped roof. This allows heavy snow to slide off. Its wooden carvings and flower boxes add beauty and colour. The mud-walled homes of the Ndebele people of South Africa keep out the hot sun. The Ndebele women often decorate the walls with colourful patterns.

Ndebele woman painting her home

Today, many people make traditional crafts for pleasure or to sell. In the past, people created these things to use them. Shops did not sell many ready-made goods. Instead, most women made their own clothes and household items. Men often made their own tools and furniture. There were no TVs or computers for entertainment. Instead, people often spent time decorating the things they made. Many people took pride in crafting useful, attractive items.

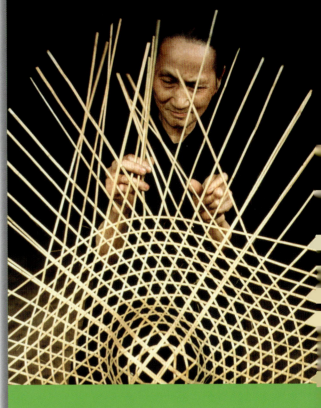

Weaving is a traditional craft. Fibres such as straw, wool or flax are used. They are woven into many things, including hats and rugs.

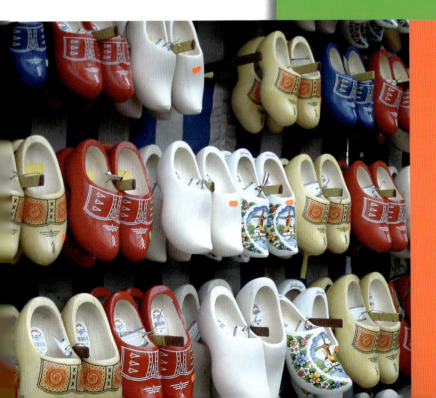

Wooden clogs are practical footwear for farmers or people who work outdoors. In Holland, some workers still wear them. Clogs keep their feet clean, dry and safe. Today, they are often painted in bright colours and sold as souvenirs.

Ancient Art, Modern Science

Ancient art teaches us about the past. From cave art, scientists work out what mattered to people thousands of years ago. Historians study **medieval** paintings. They use them to see how people used to dress and live.

Experts work to repair and protect old art. If they didn't do so, it would be lost forever. The science of repairing art is called art restoration. Art **conservation**, on the other hand, protects art from future damage. Some restorers and conservators work on huge ancient monuments. Others work on small paintings. There is great skill involved in restoration and conservation. Workers must protect the art. They must also keep it as close to its original form as possible.

The Great Sphinx was covered in scaffolding for much of the 1990s. About 100,000 stones were used to repair it.

In 1940, four French teenagers discovered some cave art at Lascaux, in southern France. The art was 17,000 years old. There are about 600 painted animals and 1500 engravings on the cavern walls. However, a spreading fungus recently threatened to destroy the art. Scientists are working to save it.

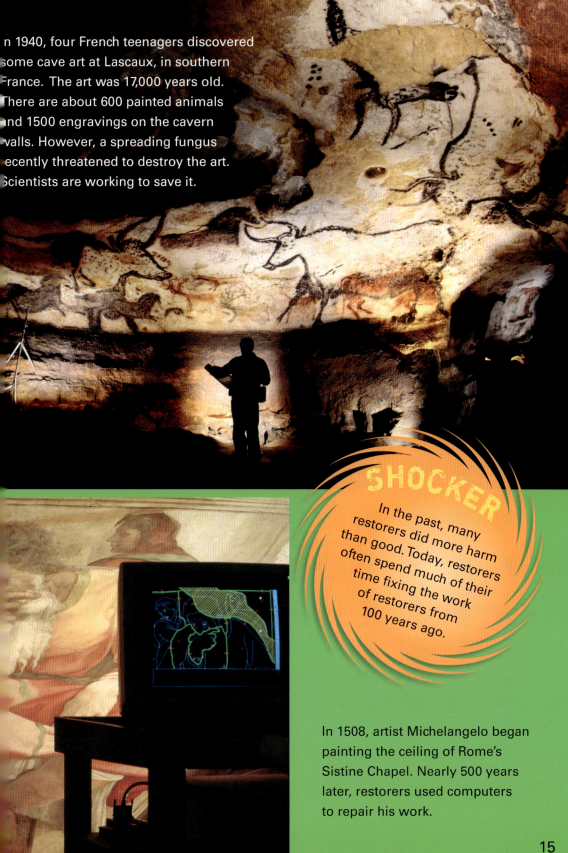

SHOCKER

In the past, many restorers did more harm than good. Today, restorers often spend much of their time fixing the work of restorers from 100 years ago.

In 1508, artist Michelangelo began painting the ceiling of Rome's Sistine Chapel. Nearly 500 years later, restorers used computers to repair his work.

Pigment and Paint

In medieval times, most people couldn't read. Religious leaders **commissioned** artworks to remind people of Bible stories. There was no photography, so rich people commissioned portraits of themselves. They wanted to be remembered after they had died.

People wanted artworks to last. It was important that the paint did not fade or flake off. Until recently, artists made their own paints. Colourful plants, soils and stones were used to make **pigments**. Some pigments were rare and expensive. For example, blue pigment was made by grinding lapis lazuli. This is a semi-precious stone. The pigment was mixed with a binder to make paint. In the **Middle Ages**, many artists painted with tempera. This had an egg-yolk binder. In the fifteenth century, oil became the binder of choice.

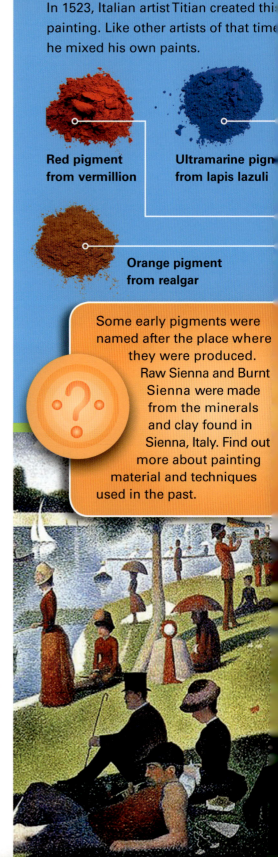

In 1523, Italian artist Titian created this painting. Like other artists of that time, he mixed his own paints.

Red pigment from vermillion

Ultramarine pigment from lapis lazuli

Orange pigment from realgar

Some early pigments were named after the place where they were produced. Raw Sienna and Burnt Sienna were made from the minerals and clay found in Sienna, Italy. Find out more about painting material and techniques used in the past.

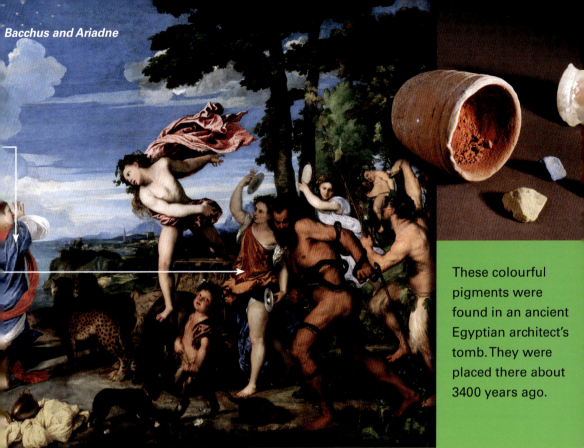

Bacchus and Ariadne

These colourful pigments were found in an ancient Egyptian architect's tomb. They were placed there about 3400 years ago.

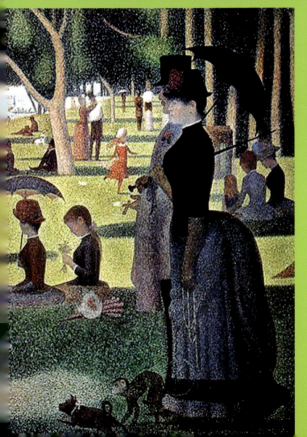

Traditionally, artists mix their colours before painting. In the late 1800s, artist Georges Seurat created colour in a new way. He put thousands of tiny coloured dots on his **canvas**. From a distance, the eye blends the colours. This creates the shades Seurat wanted the viewer to see.

Seurat's *Sunday Afternoon on the Island of La Grande Jatte*, 1886

Seurat's style is called pointillism. From close up, the viewer can see the tiny coloured dots.

17

The Tools of the Trade

This X-ray image shows how the artist Titian changed the position of a woman's head. Both heads are shown in the X-ray image.

Conservators and restorers need to fix and clean artworks without harming them. To do this, they often use special tools. They use microscopes to get a close look. They also use techniques involving **infrared rays**, **X-rays** and **lasers**.

In X-radiography, art experts produce images the same way as doctors make X-rays of bones. X-rays are fired at a painting. Depending on the thickness of the paint and the kinds of paint used, more or fewer X-rays pass through the painting. Those that get through strike photographic paper on the other side. This creates an image. The image provides information about all the paint layers in a painting.

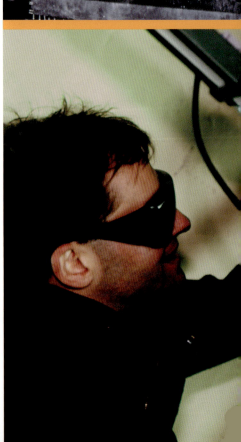

Infrared rays reach deeper into a painting than ordinary light rays. In one technique, infrared light is used to see if there are pencil or charcoal marks under the paint. The infrared light is shone onto the painting. Special cameras pick up the infrared light that reflects off the painting. Any black marks under the paint appear black on screen. This is because the chemicals in the pencil or charcoal do not reflect the infrared light.

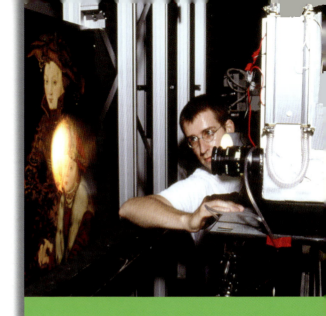

An infrared scanner moves across a painting. The whole painting is scanned. Then the machine produces a black-and-white image. It reveals any sketches beneath the paint.

Conservators often use lasers to clean sculptures and carved stone. The lasers produce powerful pulses of infrared light. This heats the dirt. It makes it expand and flake off.

○ **Uncleaned stone**
○ **Cleaned stone**

Organising the information helps me to compare the different techniques.

Tool	Characteristic	Purpose
X-radiography	X-rays pass through painting	To gather information about paint layers
Infrared rays	Rays reflect off some surfaces	To see pencil lines under the paint
Lasers	Produce pulses that heat dirt	To clean sculptures and carved stone

19

Fake!

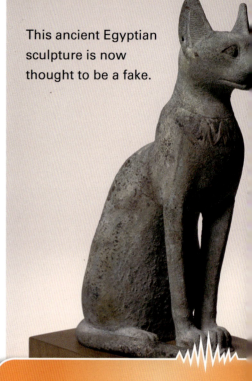

This ancient Egyptian sculpture is now thought to be a fake.

Artworks by famous artists sell for millions of pounds. As do very old artworks. Therefore, many people have tried to create fake artworks. Often it is very hard to tell what is real and what is not. Experts use many techniques to uncover the fakes. One useful technique is called X-ray diffraction. Tiny samples of paint are analysed using X-rays. This technique reveals a sample's exact chemical content.

Portrait of a Woman (below right) was once thought to have been painted by the Spanish artist Francisco Goya. X-ray diffraction of a speck of white paint showed that it was zinc white. This paint was invented after Goya died. An X-radiograph of the painting showed another painting underneath. The cracks in the original painting had been used to make the fake painting look old.

There are many English words with similar meanings to the word *fake*. Some of them are: *forgery*, *fraud*, *counterfeit*, *bogus*, *false* and *phony*.

Face that was under the forged face

Face once thought to have been painted by Goya

Some of the techniques used to study masterpieces are also used to detect forgeries. For example, many paintings are examined under **ultraviolet (UV) light**. The UV light makes some paints **fluoresce**. The amount of fluorescence depends on the pigments and their age. This helps the experts work out which pigments were used.

THE MASTER FORGER

Han van Meegeren was a famous Dutch forger. During World War II, he created six paintings. They were supposedly by the seventeenth-century Dutch painter Johannes Vermeer. He sold the paintings to German officers for huge sums of money. The fakes were hard to detect. Van Meegeren had used mainly pigments available when Vermeer was alive in the 1600s. He also used old canvases. However, chemical analysis showed that the paints contained a modern plastic binder. It had not been invented in Vermeer's time.

This forgery was examined under UV light. Dark blotches showed up. They revealed where the paint had been retouched.

This is van Meegeren at his trial in 1947. One of his forged paintings is hanging behind him.

SHOCKER

In 1496, artist Michelangelo forged an ancient Roman carving. It was sold to a religious leader. The man was furious when he learned the truth. However, he was also impressed.

Art and Maths

The branch of maths that involves studying shapes is called geometry. It involves 2-D shapes. These include squares, triangles and circles. It also involves 3-D forms. These include cubes, pyramids and spheres. When these shapes are combined in repetitive ways, they create patterns. The artist MC Escher created fascinating images by linking 2-D shapes in patterns with no gaps. These patterns are called **tessellations**.

Another kind of artwork created using the rules of maths is a **fractal**. Each fractal is actually a graph of a maths equation. Computers are needed to create complex fractal images.

Tessellation by MC Escher

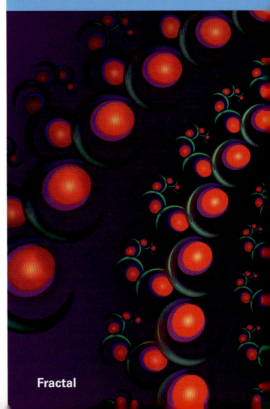

Fractal

Geometry	
2-D Shapes	**3-D Forms**
square	cube
triangle	pyramid
circle	sphere

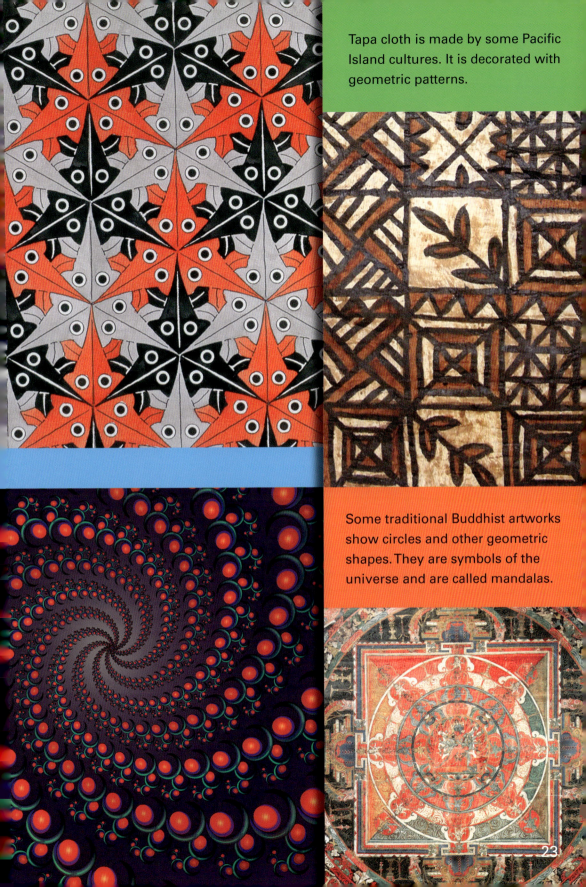

Tapa cloth is made by some Pacific Island cultures. It is decorated with geometric patterns.

Some traditional Buddhist artworks show circles and other geometric shapes. They are symbols of the universe and are called mandalas.

The Art of Illusion

To paint a realistic scene, an artist must master the art of **perspective**. Some artists have twisted the rules of perspective. They create illusions that fool the mind. This kind of art is called optical art, or op art. Some op-art images seem to make sense until you look closely. Some appear to be 3-D. Others look as if they are moving. Artists create these images using repetition of simple forms. The forms often include circles and **parallel** lines.

Vega-Nor by Victor Vasarely, 1969

Waterfall by MC Escher, 1961. Does the water flow along a flat surface or upward

PERSPECTIVE

Artists often imagine lines coming out of an object to meet at one or more points in the distance. This helps them achieve realistic angles.

One-point perspective

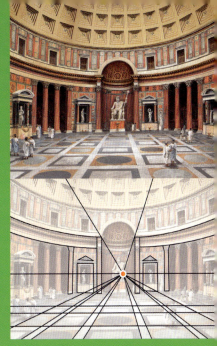

One-point perspective

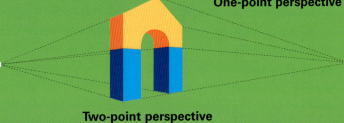

Two-point perspective

Is this image really moving, or does it just appear to move?

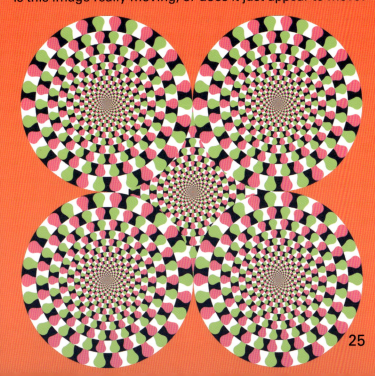

Technology and Art

As technology has advanced, so has art. No sooner had photography and film been invented than artists began to use these new media. Film makers and computer-game creators constantly push technology to its limits. Today, special effects are often created using computers. Techno-wizards transform ordinary film scenes into magical fantasy worlds. They work to make their animated characters more and more realistic. Production companies compete to make each new film more spectacular than the last.

Techno-wizard is a new word. It is used to describe people who are clever at using technology. Some related words are: *techno-fear*, *techno-mall*, *techno-geek*, *techno-stress*.

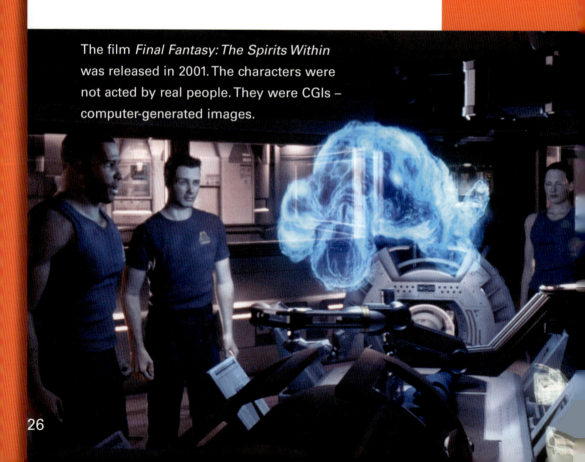

The film *Final Fantasy: The Spirits Within* was released in 2001. The characters were not acted by real people. They were CGIs – computer-generated images.

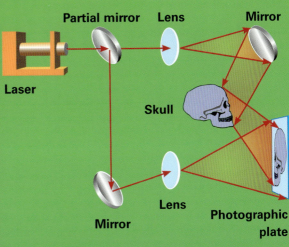

MAKING A HOLOGRAM

uch twentieth-century art was experimental.
w techniques were mixed with old ones.
this 1963 portrait of Jacqueline Kennedy,
ist Andy Warhol enlarged a photo. He then
ered it using coloured inks.

A hologram is a 3-D image. It is made using laser light. The laser beam is split into two beams. One beam shines on a photographic plate. The other beam bounces off the object and then onto the plate. Where the two beams meet, a pattern forms on the plate. When the plate is developed, a 3-D image appears. It seems to hover in front of the plate.

Front view   **Side view**

This holographic skull featured on the November 1985 cover of *National Geographic* magazine. The viewer sees slightly different views of the skull when looking from different angles.

27

Music and Much More

Music is another field that combines art and science. Many instruments have notes that go up in steps. Scientists know that each note makes the air **vibrate** at a particular rate per second. Today, machines can create these tones electronically. Musicians use computers and machines called synthesisers to compose music. They can create almost any sound they can imagine. However, just like all musicians, they still need talent to create good music.

A piece of music can be translated into a form of writing. For hundreds of years, people have used musical notation to write down their **compositions**.

Architecture, film and music are just some of the fields where art and science support each other. Take a look at the world around you. How are the things you can see influenced by the worlds of art and science? The page you are looking at right now is just one example.

Science photographer

Here are some careers that combine art and science:

- Science photographer
- Computer animator
- Art restorer
- Computer-game creator
- Architect
- Fashion designer
- Graphic artist

DID YOU KNOW?

People have been writing music for thousands of years. The first-known written music is about 4500 years old. It came from the Middle East.

Computer animator

Talented DJs can mix music and sounds digitally at a club, while people are dancing.

29

Some people think that they can't be good at both **logic**-based subjects and creative subjects. However, geniuses such as Leonardo da Vinci show us that this is not true. In fact, many ordinary people have careers that combine art and science.

WHAT DO YOU THINK?

Should secondary-school students be allowed to specialise in just the arts or the sciences?

PRO

There is too much information available these days for everyone to know about everything. We need to specialise. Also, students will enjoy school and stay longer if they can do the things they enjoy.

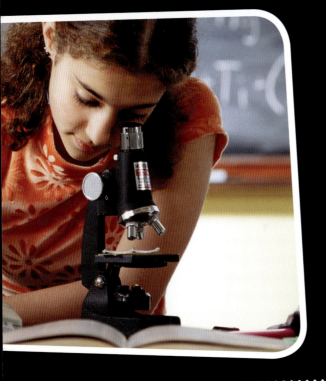

At many secondary schools, students choose their subjects. Some do mainly science. Others do mainly arts. This helps them prepare for certain college courses, but it also means they stop learning in one area or the other.

CON

I think people limit themselves and their futures too soon. We should all have a broad education. That way, we will be able to combine scientific and artistic ideas as adults. It will keep our brains active and make us more interesting people.

Go to **www.tessellations.org** to learn more about art and science.

GLOSSARY

cathedral the main church in an area

composition a complex piece of music

conservation the process of protecting artworks and other valuable objects from damage

fluoresce to give off light, or to glow, when energy is absorbed

infrared ray an energy ray with a slightly longer wavelength than visible light. We feel some infrared rays as heat.

laser a machine that produces a narrow, powerful beam of light of a particular wavelength

logic thinking that involves reasoning and following steps to reach correct answers

masterpiece an outstanding work of art or craft

medieval to do with the Middle Ages

Middle Ages the period in European history from about AD 500 to about AD 1500.

parallel two lines that are always exactly the same distance apart and never meet or cross

Renaissance a period in European history that lasted from the 1300s until about 1600. The Renaissance (meaning "rebirth") was marked by advances in art, literature and science.

restorer a person who fixes damaged artworks or other valuable objects

tradition something, such as a belief or a craft, that is handed down through generations

ultraviolet light energy rays with a shorter wavelength than visible light. Ultraviolet, or UV, rays make some materials fluoresce.

vibrate to move back and forth at a very fast pace

X-ray an energy ray with a much shorter wavelength than visible light. X-rays can pass through some solid objects but not others.

INDEX

Alberti, Leon Battista	8	light	19, 2?
architecture	6–8, 10–12, 29	maths	7–8, 10, 22–2?
art conservation	14, 18–19	music	28–2?
art restoration	7, 14–15, 18, 29	op art	24–2?
crafts	13	perspective	24–2?
da Vinci, Leonardo	6, 30	pigments	16–17, 2?
films	26, 29	Renaissance	8
forgery	20–21	sculptures	8–9, 19–2?
fractals	22	technology	12, 26–2?
geometry	22–23	tessellations	2?
infrared rays	18–19	UV light	2?
lasers	18–19, 27	X-rays	18–2?

32